# The Secrets
# of Finishing Hooked Rugs

by Margaret Siano with Susan Huxley

**Happy Time Bears,** 36" x 24", #6-cut wool on linen.
Designed by Jane McGown Flynn (The House of Price).
Hooked by Cathy Edwards, Phillipsburg, New Jersey, 2001.

---

## DEDICATION

*To all my rug hooking friends and family,*
*whose encouragement and assistance*
*made this book possible.*

## RUG HOOKING WORKSHOP SERIES

## The Secrets of Finishing Hooked Rugs

*by Margaret Siano with Susan Huxley*

**Editor**
*Wyatt R. Myers*

**Book Designer**
*Cher Williams*

**Assistant Editor**
*Lisa McMullen*

**Chairman**
*M. David Detweiler*

**Publisher**
*J. Richard Noel*

**Content produced by the**
*Sew 'n Tell Studio, Easton, Pennsylvania*

**Substantive Editor and Photo Stylist**
*Susan Huxley*

**Proofreader**
*Oli Landwijt*

**Photographer**
*Robert Gerheart*

*Presented by*

R·U·G HOOKING

1300 Market St., Suite 202
Lemoyne, PA 17043-1420
(717) 234-5091 • (800) 233-9055
*www.rughookingonline.com*
*rughook@paonline.com*

PRINTED IN CHINA

# Table of Contents

# From the Editor

As rug hooking artists, you all understand and appreciate the depth and intricacy that hooked art can achieve. At the same time, however, the act of hooking itself is actually quite simple. Stick your hook through the backing fabric, pull up a loop, and that's all there is to it.

Most rug hookers would agree, however, that one technical aspect of the craft gives even the most seasoned artist headaches from time to time: finishing your hand-hooked work.

For as many rug hookers as there are in this world, an equal number of ways exist for finishing a rug. Some prefer whip-stitching (with or without cording), some prefer a simple application of rug tape, and still others take it to an intricate level, by braiding borders, crocheting edges, or adding fringe.

And while we can't cover EVERY finishing technique in one book, we'd like to think we came about as close as you can get in one publication.

So it is with great pride that we introduce *The Secrets of Finishing Hooked Rugs* by Margaret Siano, the most comprehensive compendium to finishing hooked rugs ever written. If you're relatively new to the craft of rug hooking, this book will be an invaluable tool. And if you're a seasoned rug hooking veteran looking to broaden your horizons or bone up on old techniques, look no further.

*The Secrets of Finishing Hooked Rugs* is just the first in a new line of continuity series books that we here at *Rug Hooking* magazine are proud to bring to you, our readers. Future books on primitive rugs and color are coming soon, and we hope they are every bit as useful to you as this book.

In the meantime, I hope this beautifully illustrated, step-by-step guide to finishing your hand-hooked masterpiece serves you well in all your hooking endeavors.

*Wyatt Myers*

## ABOUT THE AUTHOR

## Margaret Siano

Margaret Siano's passion for rug hooking began almost four decades ago, under the guidance of renowned hooker Alice Beatty.

Her work has appeared in print many times, including the cover of a telephone directory. Her commissions come from collectors across the country and as far away as Japan. She's even held a 40-rug, one-woman show at the Princeton Medical Center in New Jersey.

In recognition of her expertise, the rug hooking community has called upon her to judge the hooked rugs at prestigious events like the Philadelphia Flower Show. In 2002, Margaret was honored with a seat on the judging panel for *A Celebration of Hand-Hooked Rugs XII*, the 2002 edition of the annual book produced by *Rug Hooking* magazine.

Despite her hectic schedule and many accolades, Margaret continues to teach private and group lessons in her studio at One Morgan Road, Flemington, NJ 08822-1902.

Margaret's business, The Hook Nook, carries rug hooking supplies, the entire collection of Lib Callaway rug designs, and her own patterns on burlap, linen, monk's cloth, and rug warp. The Hook Nook welcomes customers by appointment only. Phone (908) 806-8083. You can visit Margaret's Web site, *www.hook-nook.com*, for product and ordering information.

# Introduction

*This book is devoted to the forgotten aspect of rug hooking.*

This may seem like a surprising statement, but when you think about it, it's really true. As rug artist Charlotte Price so eloquently puts it, *"Rug hookers spend endless hours on the details of making a hooked piece; We measure our dyes precisely; we make sure we have perfect values; and we develop a finely honed hooking technique. But after the loops and colors are correct and the hooking is completed, we either roll the rug up and store it or rush through the final steps. It is true that color is the first element that draws us to the rug. The technique may then come into play in the presentation. But if the rug is not finished with the same exacting standards as were put into the other two elements of the rug, the quality of the piece is diminished."*

Truer words on the topic of rug hooking have never been spoken. After hours of precise, detailed work on your hand-hooked masterpiece, your method for finishing the rug may seem like an afterthought. But it's not: The technique you use to finish your rug is almost as important as the hooking itself. After the beautiful interior of the work, what do you think the rug's admirer is going to notice next?

The interesting thing about finishing a hooked rug, in fact, is that for something that is often considered an afterthought, there are hundreds of ways to do it! Whipping, rug tape, binding, braiding, crocheting, adding fringe: The possibilities are so boundless that it is nearly impossible to cover them all in one book! But this book comes closer to covering every finishing technique than anything previously published.

As Charlotte Price goes on to say, *"Shoddy work makes a statement about both the technician and the recipient of the hooked item."* With the precise, detailed, step-by-step instructions and photographs found only in *The Secrets of Finishing Hooked Rugs*, your finished rug will be sure to make the right statement.

Even if your friend's or teacher's finishing technique is not your cup of tea, this book has an option that will work for you. Thirteen finishing techniques are covered in the same exquisite detail: You'll just love the completeness of this book. And to admire the finished results of all these beautiful finishing techniques, be sure to flip to the bonus "Finished Rug Gallery," starting on page 47.

*The Secrets of Finishing Hooked Rugs* is truly your complete guide to finishing a hand-hooked rug. To see for yourself, turn the page to a bold new world of finishing techniques. Once you see the completeness of techniques in this book, you won't want to finish a rug without it!

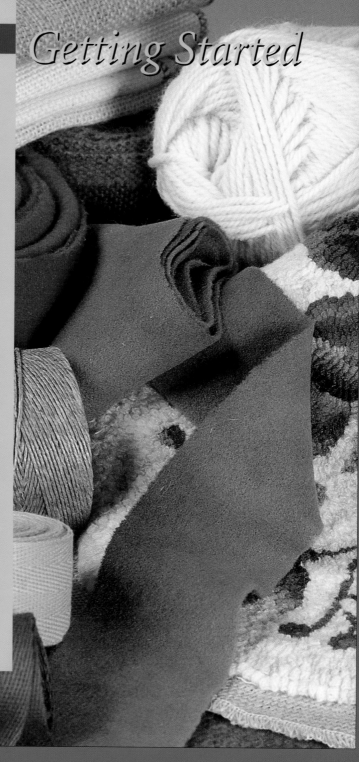

# CHAPTER ONE

# Getting Started

*Welcome to the beginning of the end. It's time to put the finishing touches on your beautiful hooked rug. As you'll see in later chapters, there are many options that will enhance your work, as well as make it more durable and valuable. But before exploring the techniques, you might want to take a look through this section, which discusses the tools that you'll need and explains any basic preparation. If you're reading this book before starting your rug . . . good for you! Decisions that you make now will leave you with more finishing choices when your rug is complete. (Make sure you check out "Plan Ahead" on page 8.)*

## Essential Equipment and Tools

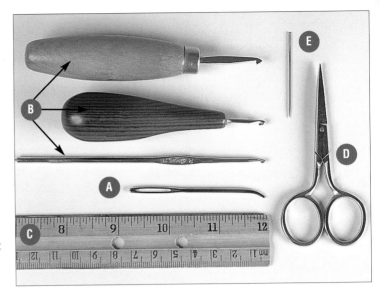

One of the things that I love about rug hooking is its simplicity. With only a few tools and supplies you can create the most gorgeous rugs. (Of course, we can go a bit crazy collecting wool, but that doesn't count.) Very little is needed to finish your first rug. You probably have everything you need right in your workbasket. Here's a summary of the items I like to have on hand:

**Carpet needle**—This is the heavy-duty needle of choice when I'm joining hooked pieces to make a larger hooked rug. The carpet needle looks like a big tapestry needle. It's longer ($2^1/2$"), has a dull point, and the eye is large enough for a wool strip.

**A. Chair and sofa needle**—Most hookers call this a bent-tip needle. It's a favorite tool for many of us because it takes so little effort to pull it through the backing. I like to use it when I'm whipping the edges of a rug. You don't need both a bent-tip needle and a tapestry needle.

**B. Hooks**—Obviously, rug hooks are one of our most important tools. A crochet hook is a must if you plan to make a crocheted edging.

**C. Ruler**—A wood ruler is shown, but yours can be clear plastic or even a tape measure. All you need is something to measure the width of a binding and the perimeter of a rug, so that you can gauge the amount of material you will need to make a binding or edging.

**D. Scissors**—Good sharp ones are the best. Make sure they aren't too large—a 1"-long blade will do the trick. You also should have a pair of larger scissors. Hookers prefer shears with offset handles to cut the tails off the wool strips in the rug.

**Serger**—This is a specialized type of sewing machine. It has a three- or four-thread stitch that prevents fabric edges from fraying. I like to serge around my backing before I start hooking. You can see the effect in the photo on page 10. But it's just as easy to use double rows of straight or zigzag machine or hand stitching for the same results. (See "Finishing Before You Start" on page 9.)

**Sewing machine**—You don't need anything fancy. In fact, you can have a beautifully finished rug that's created with little more than hand stitching. But a sewing machine can save you time. You can use its straight stitch to baste cording inside a wool strip, permanently sew one edge of a binding to the backing, and also to quickly join the short ends of wool strips to make a longer piece that will fit the rug's perimeter.

**E. Sharp hand-sewing needle**—I'm not too particular about the type and size of needle that I use. As long as the all-purpose sewing thread fits through the eye, I'm happy. A hand-sewing needle is used for simple steps like basting, straight stitching binding to backing, or sewing together the beginning and end of a strip that's almost completely attached to the rug.

**Tapestry needle**—I have a couple of these but usually bypass them in favor of a bent-tip needle. When I do need a tapestry needle, I prefer a dull point size 18. You don't need both a bent-tip needle and a tapestry needle.

# Backing Basics

Like the style of rugs that catch your eye, you probably have a favorite backing. Every backing has its merits, which are based on the type of fiber that it's made from. My goal in this section isn't to sway your choice by discussing the merits of each type. Instead, I'd like to explain how the characteristics of your backing might affect the results of the finishing technique that you choose.

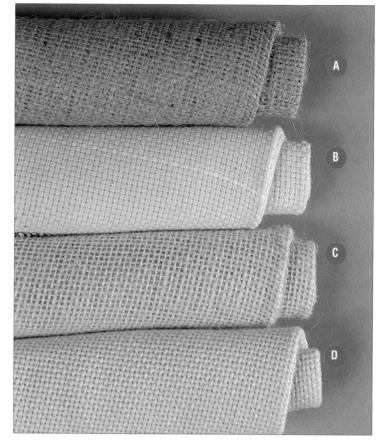

**A. Burlap**—Also called jute, burlap has a limited life. It has to be treated carefully. Mind you, I've repaired some antique burlap rugs that have worn very well. The best survivors had a cotton binding. Self binding didn't do well at all.

When I was learning to hook, Alice Beatty told me I had to hand-sew when finishing a burlap backing. I didn't, and thought I had pulled one over on the teacher. Ten years later, I knew I was wrong. It looked like a razor had sliced through the fragile backing along the line of machine stitching.

A rug's edges seem to be the part of the rug that suffers first, so a suitable finish will protect this area of the backing. I wouldn't use self binding because folding the burlap stresses the fibers and exposes the outer fold to considerable wear and tear. I prefer a corded edging for burlap rugs because this finish has a bumper. However, you can apply any of the bindings and edgings in this book to burlap.

Despite its tendency to fray, when you prepare burlap for finishing (See "Finishing Before You Start" on page 9), there's no need to leave additional excess backing. The two rows of stitching will prevent fraying.

**B. Monk's Cloth**—This cotton backing is friendly and soft. Since it's flexible, finishing the rug is easier. Unfortunately, this attribute is also a drawback because large pieces have a tendency to stretch. I like monk's cloth because evenly spaced vertical lines are worked into the weave. Any finishing technique can be applied to this backing.

**C. Linen**—You're going to put a lot of time and effort into a piece, so you'll want it to last a long time. Linen will outlast all of us. Its durable nature makes it suitable for any finish that you want to try. Although it costs substantially more than burlap, linen is strong and easy to hook.

**D. Rug Warp**—Although used commercially, rug warp isn't as popular among hookers. Like monk's cloth, rug warp is cotton. But rug warp is heavier, so it doesn't stretch as much. This backing is suitable for all finishes presented in *The Secrets of Finishing Hooked Rugs*.

## Plan Ahead

The way that you finish your rug can be decided at almost any stage. But if you want to keep your options open, it's best to make a few decisions before you pull the first loop through the backing.

■ **Leave a lot.** If you're thinking about the ultimate luxury—framing your finished rug—don't trim your backing close to the pattern. It's best to leave at least 6" outside beyond the outer edges of the border.

■ **Shop at one stop.** It's easier to select matching or color-coordinated materials for the edging or backing if you pick them out at the same time you're choosing the colors and textures for the hooking strips.

■ **Bind first.** If you want a cotton binding, then you need to apply it before you even begin hooking. The inner edge of the binding needs to be as close as possible to the outermost row of hooking. Applying the binding first is the best way to achieve these results.

■ **Buy more.** Some finishing techniques, like the braided edging (see page 22), take more yardage. Another example is a flat wool binding, which needs $2^1/2$"-wide wool strips. It's best to have a bit left over, rather than run short. After all, those leftover snippets can be used elsewhere.

■ **Consider alternatives.** A crocheted edging looks super when it's the same fabric as the hooked border. But, if you used textured wool for the border, you may not be happy using it for crocheting. Textured fabric tends to fray more.

■ **Avoid a bind.** Ideally, you need 6" of excess backing around all edges of the rug that will be finished with a self binding. Start with even more excess backing, to allow for fraying and wear-and-tear.

■ **Knot enough.** Purchase extra yarn so that a rug fringe is made from the same material that you used to whip the edges.

▶**TIP** **Nix the Covering**

It's tempting to sew a cloth over the backing of the finished rug. The desire to protect your treasure is admirable, albeit misguided. Dirt will be trapped between the covering and the backing. It acts as an abrasive that wears down the rug. In the same vein, I know some women who like to cover up patches, but this also adds to the destruction.

## Finishing Before You Start

Whatever backing you work on, you need to prevent it from raveling while you're handling the rug during the subsequent finishing. There are several methods for treating the edges of a backing (see "A Stitch in Time" on page 10). Hookers usually choose one and stick with it.

As you browse through this book, you might notice that some of the rug photos clearly show a backing that's finished with only a single row of straight stitching. Without looking at the credits, you can be sure that these rugs aren't mine. They were made by friends kind enough to share their ideas with you.

I prefer to serge the edges of my backing (see photo C on page 10), but not everyone can afford the luxury of having one of these specialized machines.

A double row of zigzag stitching is my second choice. In the following steps, I explain this method. You'll probably find the process familiar because you may have done something similar to a backing before you started hooking it.

### Supplies

- #14 sharp sewing machine needle
- All-purpose sewing thread, color-matched to the binding*
- Scissors
- Sewing machine with zigzag stitch

*For clarity, contrasting thread is used for the step-by-step photos. It's best to use color-matched thread on your rug.

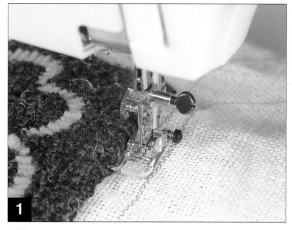

**1** Set your machine for a medium-length (about 10 stitches per inch) and medium-width zigzag stitch. Make a line of stitching 1/2" from the last row that you hooked. Stitch along one edge of the rug, parallel to the last row of hooking. (*The following steps are shown on linen, but the same process applies to all types of backing.*)

**2** Shift the backing so that you're back at the start. The right edge of the presser foot should be beside the first line of stitching. Make a second line of zigzag stitching parallel to the first.

**3** Cut off the excess backing that's beyond the first, outermost line of zigzag stitching. Don't cut too close to the stitching; otherwise it will "fall" off the edge if the backing frays. Don't worry about cutting the backing in a perfectly straight line. As you finish your rug, this edge will be folded underneath or hidden under a binding.

You have other options for preparing edges: hand stitching, machine straight stitching, and serging. While hand stitching has definite advantages when working with burlap backing, the remaining alternatives are a matter of personal preference.

**A** Hand stitching is a great option if you don't have a sewing machine. It's also my preferred method when I'm working with burlap. The hand stitches are gentler on this fragile backing. The hand-stitching process is the same as making machine zigzag stitches, which is explained on page 9. But, as the photo at right shows, use a doubled length of all-purpose sewing thread, and place the second stitching line as close as possible to the first. Make each stitch no more than 1/4" long.

**B** Machine straight stitching is positioned exactly the same way that you place zigzag stitches. You can follow the same steps on page 9 with the machine set for a medium-length straight stitch. You can see the results in the photo at right. Honestly, I can't recommend straight stitching because I think zigzag stitches are stronger.

**C** Serging is fast and easy after you've mastered this specialized type of sewing machine. The machine cuts off the excess backing at the same time that it stitches the edge. It also works best for all backings. I like this edge finish so much that I bought a machine just to prepare backings for me and my customers. In fact, I serge the edges of my patterns before they're hooked. Use a three- or four-thread, medium-length and medium- or wide-width overlock stitch.

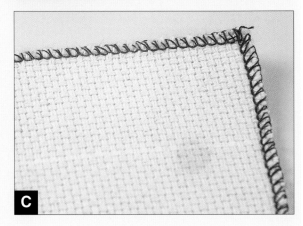

# CHAPTER TWO

# Beginning with Bindings

You have almost finished your work of art, and now it's the time to complete the edges. This chapter will show you better ways to accomplish this.

Whatever the finishing plans for your rug, there's a very good chance that you'll start with one of three basic bindings: self, cotton, or flat wool binding. All are explained in detail on the following pages.

Even though these bindings are rather basic, that doesn't make them any less attractive. Even very special rugs can be finished with a humble self binding. (The rug in this photo was designed by Jane McGown Flynn and hooked by Norma McElhenny using #3-cut wool on burlap.)

## Self Binding

This is the most common finish for rugs that have straight edges. It's also a great first step if you want to attach an edging. Lauri Rubinetti, who designed and hooked *Poor Kitty,* shown in the photo, made a self binding and then completed her rug with a luxurious braided edging.

You could self bind a round rug, but I wouldn't recommend it because the underside would be too bulky. Self binding also isn't the best choice for burlap, and rugs that are round, oval, or scalloped.

These cautions aside, this is an excellent finish because it's so easy. Even though you won't make the self binding until the rug is completely hooked, you must plan for extra backing beyond all edges of the finished hooking. Ideally, you need a little over 6" for the process. The edges of the backing will probably be subjected to some wear and tear during the hooking, so you should start with at least 8" of excess backing beyond the hooked border.

### Supplies

- All-purpose sewing thread, color-matched to backing
- Button & carpet (heavy-duty) thread, color-matched to the rug
- Hand-sewing needle
- Iron
- Ruler
- Scissors
- Sewing machine
- Towel

### ▶TIP  Buy the Yard

Cotton binding is sold by the yard, so you don't need to join pieces to make the binding long enough for the entire rug's perimeter. Before buying the yardage, measure around the outer edge of the rug's border. You're going to need more than this because the beginning and end of the binding will overlap. It's also a good idea to get a bit extra just in case you make a mistake. I usually buy an extra 6".

**1** Decide upon the desired finished width of the self binding. I would never make the width less than 1". The most common width is in the 2" to 3" range. Around all edges of the rug, cut the backing to twice the desired finished width. In this example, I cut 6" from the last row of hooking, so that the finished self binding will be 3" wide. Before cutting off the excess backing, remember to stitch near the cutting line to prevent the edge of the backing from fraying. (See "Finishing Before You Start" on page 9.) Choose a starting point that isn't near a corner. Working along one edge and with the rug wrong side up, fold the edge of the backing so that it butts against the last row of hooking.

**2** Still working on one side of the rug, fold the backing a second time so that all of the backing is on the wrong side of the rug. The backing naturally folds along the edge of the hooking. From the right side, you shouldn't be able to see any backing along the edge.

**3** Thread the needle with an arm's length piece of doubled thread and knot together the ends. Working along the inner folded edge, sew the inner edge of the backing to the wrong side of the rug. Start near one corner. I

like to use an overcast stitch, but you can use a blindstitch or a whipstitch. (See page 57 for stitch instructions.) Dig into the backing to make sure that your needle grabs enough of the rug wool for secure stitching.

**4** Hand sew along the edge. As you near the corner, stop stitching and prepare the miter. Make the first fold on the second side of the rug by butting the edge of the backing against the last row of hooking. Maintaining the double fold along the first edge, tuck under the corner. Now make the second fold along the second side of the rug, so that all of the backing is on the wrong side of the rug.

**5** For the time being, ignore the diagonal fold. Continue stitching the backing to the rug along the first—and then the second—side of the rug. Fold and miter the remaining sides and corners as you stitch around the rest of the rug.

**6** Place the rug, still wrong side up, on a hard surface with a towel underneath. Place a damp towel on top. Using a dry iron at medium to high heat (the wool setting), press the backing and the miters. As I work, I lift the iron from spot to spot, but you can slide it along the surface, if desired. Leave the rug in position to dry.

**7** Secure the miter by stitching along the folded edge. If desired, you can give all of the miters a second pressing. Now that the finish is complete, block the rug by following the instructions on page 59.

## Cotton Binding

This finish is less bulky than the self binding, but there are a few more steps. Nevertheless, it's the most common rug finish. It's a nice alternative if you scrimped around the edges because the backing for your rug was expensive. And it'll save your bacon if you accidentally end up with only a little backing beyond the hooked outer border. You need very little space—not even 1/4"—since the binding goes right next to the outermost loops.

Sharon Ballard, who hooked the Lib Callaway design shown, was wise to use the cotton binding because the rug has burlap backing.

I was trained to attach one side of the cotton binding to the backing before I hook the rug. You can attach the binding after completely hooking the rug, but it's much easier and more attractive if you do it sooner. At the very least, the binding should be attached before you finish hooking the border.

### Supplies

- Cotton binding*
- Scissors
- All-purpose sewing thread, color-matched to the binding (optional, for machine stitching)
- Button & carpet (heavy-duty) thread
- Sewing machine (optional, see "Cuts Like A Knife" on page 16).
- Hand-sewing needle

*The standard 1 1/4" width is sold by the yard.

### ▶TIP  Big is Beautiful

I'm in the finishing stages of a 10' x 12' rug. I'm sure you can imagine the weight of such a large rug. My husband, Dick, helps me move it around. When I'm stitching, I use several kitchen chairs to support the weight. I know some hookers who stitch by simply sitting on the floor with the heavy rug in their lap.

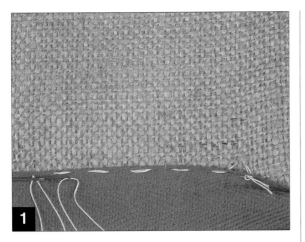

**1** Choose a starting point that isn't near a corner. With right sides facing, place the cotton binding on top of the rug. Shift the binding to the outermost lengthwise edge on the pattern line (or no more than 1/4" from the outer edge of the pattern's border, where the outermost edge of the hooking will be). The entire binding width should be on the pattern—not the excess—side of the backing. Sew the outermost lengthwise edge of the binding to the backing around all sides of the pattern. Your stitching method depends on the backing (see "Cuts Like a Knife" below).

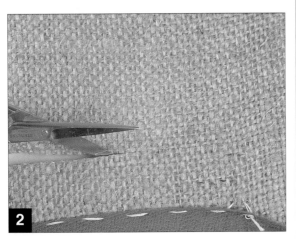

**2** You no longer need the extra backing that's beyond the outer edge of the cotton binding. Cut off this excess backing. I like to trim it to 3/4" wide, as measured from the closest edge of the binding. At this width, the excess backing won't show when the binding is finished. If desired, before cutting the backing, stitch the edge just inside the planned cutting line to raveling (see "Finishing Before You Start" on page 9).

**3** Flip the binding right side up, folding it away from the pattern printed on the backing. The binding may not lay flat at the corners. This is fine. Complete the rug, hooking as close as possible to the binding. When completely hooked, no backing should be visible between the outermost loops and the inner, attached edge of the binding.

▶ **TIP Cuts Like a Knife**

The step 1 and 2 photos on the left show the binding hand stitched to the burlap backing with heavy-duty thread and a running stitch. You can machine-straight stitch a binding to any backing except burlap. Machine stitching will eventually slice through the fragile burlap fibers. To machine stitch other backings, use a medium-length straight stitch.

**4** Fold the binding to the wrong side of the rug. With doubled heavy-duty thread, hand sew the inner edge of the binding to the rug. Don't start at a corner, and catch only a thread of the backing in each stitch. I like to use an overcast stitch, but you can use a blindstitch or a whipstitch. (See page 57 for stitch instructions.)

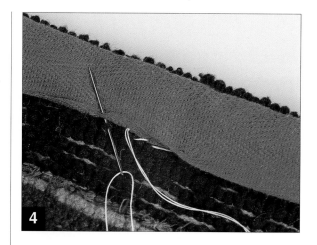

**5** Hand sew along the first edge. As you near the corner, stop stitching and prepare the miter. Fold the binding to the wrong side along the second edge of the rug. Maintaining the fold along the first edge, tuck the corner underneath the folded binding at the start of the second edge. (For additional guidance, look at the photo with step 4 of "Self Binding," on page 13.)

**6** For the time being, ignore the diagonal fold. Continue stitching the backing to the rug along the first—and then the second—side of the rug. In the same manner, fold and miter the binding along the remaining corners and sides of the rug. Back at the beginning, cut off the binding so that the raw end can be turned under and still overlap the start of the work. Finish attaching the binding by sewing the end of the binding and the diagonal fold for every miter. (The step 7 photo for "Self Binding," on page 14, shows a stitched miter.)

## Flat Wool Binding

I used to spend a lot of time repairing the edges of antique rugs. Edges are the first thing that are damaged. To help rugs survive longer, I encourage students to use a flat wool edging. With this finish, the edge of the hooking is protected by a bumper wool-encased cording. A wool strip is wrapped around cording and then rolled from front to back. You can use a flat wool binding for any type of backing.

*Nantucket Scallop*, a Lib Callaway design that's hooked by Norma McElhenny in the photo, is a striking example. You might think it's more difficult to work with a scalloped or round rug, but this isn't the case.

On a square or rectangular rug, it's easy to miter the binding that's on the underside. But it isn't possible to miter the corded bumper. You'll have to practice a bit to develop a feel for working around a corner so that the finished point will lie flat.

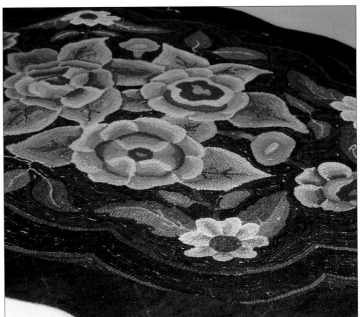

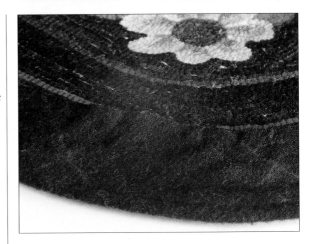

### Supplies

- 2¹/₂"- to 3"-wide background wool, 6" longer than rug's perimeter*
- All-purpose sewing thread and sewing machine (optional, see step 4)
- Bent-tip, carpet, or tapestry needle
- Button & carpet (heavy-duty) thread, color-matched to wool strip
- Cotton or synthetic cording 6" longer than the rug's perimeter
- Hand-sewing needle

*To make a continuous strip, join shorter lengths with a diagonal seam (see page 58).*

### ▶ TIP  Size to Fit

Cording with a ¹/₈" diameter is good for a finely hooked rug, while a ¹/₄" diameter is best for a primitive rug.

**1** The excess backing, beyond the outer edge of the hooking, needs to be stitched and then trimmed before attaching the binding. (See "Finishing Before You Start" on page 9.) Cut off the excess backing 3/4" to 1" from the outer edge of the hooking. In the step-by-step photos, the backing is serged. Use double rows of zigzag stitching on your backing.

**2** If necessary, join short pieces of binding to make a length that's long enough to go around the rug's perimeter. See page 58 for instructions to join two pieces.

**3** Place the cording on the wrong side of the wool strip, with the beginning of the cording 3" from the start of the strip. (You need the extra wool to join the beginning and end of the strips, as explained in step 5.) Wrap one lengthwise edge of the strip around the cording. Don't match the long edges. Let the side that's on top, which was folded, extend only 1/4" beyond the cording. This side (with the shorter edge) will be visible when the rug is finished and placed on the floor. Pin together the long edges. Install a zipper foot on your sewing machine and straight stitch the sides as pinned, starting and ending at the ends of the cording. Don't catch the cording in the stitching. If desired, you can hand sew with a hand-sewing needle and all-purpose sewing thread.

**4** With the rug right side up, place the binding face down on top, with the corded edge toward the hooking. Align the straight stitching on the binding with the edge of the hooking. Place the start of the binding anywhere but at a corner. Fold the excess backing (beyond the last hooked edge) and binding to the underside. Pin it in place. Don't fold the corded edge to the underside. Instead, let it extend beyond the rug.

**▶TIP Round Cord on a Square Rug**

Don't worry about mitering the corded edge as you sew it to the backing. Just "push" a little extra cording and binding into the corner so that the finished corner doesn't curl. In the next step, you need to miter the binding that's on the underside of the rug. To make a miter, see steps 4 to 7 of "Self Binding" on pages 13 and 14.

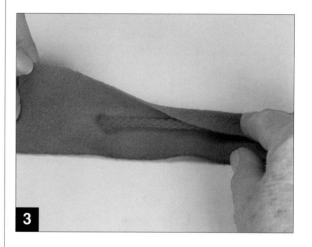

**5** Using a doubled length of heavy-duty thread, one of the larger needles, and starting 2" from the beginning of the cording (5" from the beginning of the binding), insert the needle into the backing as close as possible to the hooked edge. No backing should be visible when the stitch is complete. Pull the needle and thread to the surface about 1/4" away. Move forward 1/4". Pull the needle and thread through the binding, between the straight stitches and cording. Continue sewing around the rug in this manner until you're back at the beginning, about 2" from the start of the hand sewing.

**6** Lift the beginning and end of the binding away from the rug. With right sides together, pin or baste the ends together. Place the joined edges against the edge of the rug to make sure the binding isn't too long or short to finish the rug's remaining edge. If necessary, adjust the joint. Sew together the ends as pinned or basted. Trim off the extra binding along the seamline. Cut off the ends of the cording so that they butt together and fit against the edge of the rug. Use doubled thread and a hand-sewing needle to stitch them together.

**7** Again using doubled heavy-duty thread, hand sew the loose, outer edge of the binding to the underside of the rug. I like to take small stitches into the backing and the underside of the binding. (The blindstitch is easier if you fold back 1/4" from the edge of the binding.) If desired, you can use an overcast stitch or whipstitch. (See page 57 for stitch instructions.)

▶**TIP** Throwing a Curve

Students making rugs with round or scalloped edges can be frustrated by the last step of the "Flat Wool Binding" because the loose edge on the rug's underside is longer than the rug's circumference. In other words, the edge of the binding has ripples. I tell them to relax and let the binding edge ripple a bit.

# CHAPTER THREE

# Enhancing with Edgings

Don't stop after you've bound the edges of your rug. Why not go the extra mile and add a border or edging? If the rug's patterns and colors lend themselves to additional embellishment, the techniques in this section of the book could be the solution. In the following pages, I'll explain how to make a braided edging, corded and whipped edging, crocheted edging, and knitted edging. Read through the instructions before hooking your rug because some treatments work best with particular backings and bindings.

# Braided Edging

A tough, often colorful, braid will protect the edges of a rug for many years. Laurie Rubinetti put a lot of thought into the border of the rug shown here. The wool strips used to make the braid pick up the red, purple, and camel featured in the rug's pattern and border. She planned to make only a single row of braid, but didn't like the effect. Thinking the braid needed to be wider, she added a second row. This still didn't look right. So she tried three rows . . . and loved the result. I do, too. This Lib Callaway *Flower and Flame* design looks great worked in complementary colors and finished with the braids.

Laurie's experimenting shows how creative thinking can lead to a good-looking rug.

If you plan to use a braided edging, work your rug on a better backing like linen, rug warp, or monk's cloth. Burlap is too weak at the edges.

## Supplies

- 1 package Braid Aids, optional*
- 1¹/₂"-wide wool strips*
- 2 large safety pins
- 3 straight dressmaker's pins
- All-purpose sewing thread, color-matched to the wool strips
- Bent-tip needle
- Clamp
- Hand-sewing needle
- Linen thread

*I like using the same wool that's in my rug. Wool flannel is the best for braiding. Textured wool, such as tweeds and plaids, look really good.*

### ▶TIP A Rose Is A Rose

Coated and uncoated linen thread is available. I haven't found the wax-like coating to be of any benefit, so use the type you prefer. This is the heaviest and strongest thread, so it does a good job holding the braid to the rug's edge. It won't show on the finished piece. Don't worry about the color.

**1** Finish the rug with a cotton or self binding, leaving about 1/4" of the excess backing exposed at the rug's edges. For the self binding, the backing should be folded to the rug's underside twice, which is the usual process. See pages 12 through 14 for complete instructions.

**2** Join the shorter wool strips to achieve the desired length. (See "The Long and Short of It" at right.) The seams can be straight or diagonal. You don't want the seams to be in the same position on all three strips, so cut off a few inches at different places at the beginning of two strips. To keep the strips under control when braiding, roll up each one separately. Stick a straight pin into the last round of each roll.

**3** Feed the start of each roll through a Braid Aid, making sure that seam allowances along a strip will be hidden inside the fold. Insert the three ends into the clamp. Start braiding, making sure that the seams are hidden. If you want to stop braiding, but fear the wool strips will untwist, insert a safety pin through the strips at the end of the braid insert.

**4** Stop when the braid is long enough to go around the entire rug, allowing 1" extra to join the beginning and end of the braid. You don't need any extra braid to traverse the corners.

▶ **TIP** The Long and Short of It

You have to do more than measure the rug's perimeter to determine the length of each wool strip you need for the braid. Even experienced hookers will figure they have enough, and then run out. As you braid the strips, each twist gobbles up a bit of additional length. The Braid Aid catalog has a table that computes the amount of wool that you need. (For a Braid Aid catalog, see the "Sources" section on page 62.)

**3**

▶ **TIP** Helping Hands

I strongly recommend using a clamp and Braid Aids. These tools make it so much easier to create even-width braids. (All are shown in the step 3 photo above.)

You need a Braid Aid for each wool strip. After you prepare the fabric, insert a short end into the wide side of the Braid Aid. When you pull the strip out through the narrow end, the strip will be folded in half with lengthwise edges inside. As you work, just slide the Braid Aid along the strip, away from the clamp. Perfect shaping every time!

A clamp will hold the start of the strips together, so that your hands are free to work with them. The type that's mounted in a stand is my favorite because it's stable and elevates the work to lap level, if you're sitting. If you don't have a clamp, put something heavy on the ends of the strips to hold them while you work.

**5** Place a safety pin through all of the strips, near the clamp. Place another safety pin at the end of the braid. Remove the braid from the clamp and place the start alongside the edge of the rug. Don't start at a corner. Place a doubled length of linen thread through a bent-tip needle and make a small stitch through the edge of the backing. Now pull the needle underneath the closest strip in the braid, 3" from the start of the braid.

**6** Pull the needle through a strand of the backing, at the edge of the rug. Continue stitching in this manner until you reach the first corner. If you didn't make a corner in the braid (see "New Twist on a Corner," page 25), ease the straight braid around the corner as you stitch it to the backing. In other words, "push" a bit of extra braid into the corner to help it lie flat when the rug is finished. When you have joined the braid to almost all of the rug's perimeter, stop sewing 3" from the end of the braid. Remove the safety pins. Take apart about 2" at the end of the braid.

**7** Insert the safety pin through the end of the braid so that it doesn't unwind more. Undo the first 2" of the start of the braid in the same manner. Unfold the end of one of the wool strips and the corresponding strip at the start of the braid. Place the strips right sides together and join them with a hand-sewing needle and doubled all-purpose thread on a hand-sewing needle. Join the remaining strips in the same manner, and then refold all of them. Place the braid against the edge of the rug to make sure that it fits. Again unfold the strips. Trim the seam allowances, refold the strips, and sew the last of the braid to the rug.

# New Twist on a Corner

You don't have to try to force a straight braid around a corner. Instead, you can make the braid turn right or left of its own accord. This involves a bit more planning. You need to carefully measure the braid to make sure the braided corners land at the rug's corners.

I usually just attach a straight braid, but this is a fun option. The following instructions explain how to make the braid turn left.

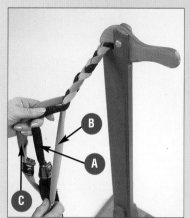

**1** Braid in the usual manner (right over left, left over right) until you reach the desired braid length to the first corner. Bring the right strip (A) over the center strip (B).

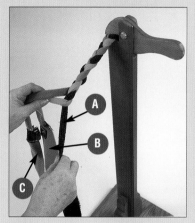

**2** Wrap strip B over strip A.

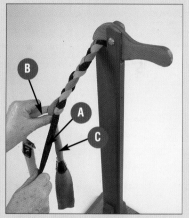

**3** Finally, wrap strip C over strip B (in the center). The corner may not be visible until you remove the braid from the clamp. Continue braiding in the usual manner to create a straight braid for the second side of the rug. Repeat these steps at each corner.

# Corded and Whipped Edging

Admittedly, the corded and whipped edging is the most time-consuming finish that you can put on a rug. But the results are well worth the extra effort. Whipping the edge creates a wonderful finish for your rug.

Hookers have used whipping to create some beautiful effects simply by changing the color of the tapestry yarn as they work around the edges of a rug. Peg Boudreau's original piece, *By the Lake*, is an excellent example. You can use colors that match the border of the rug or mingle several strands to create a variegated effect. On one of my rugs, I had the tapestry yarn hand-dyed to match the colors in the border and background.

I also like this edging because it builds in a cord bumper that protects the edge of the rug. Some people put the cording on the back of the rug, but I prefer placing it on the front.

Whipping is suitable for all backings. Shapes are another matter. For example, it would be difficult—but not impossible—on a rug with a scalloped edge.

## ▶TIP The Skinny on Cording

The diameter of your cording should match the height of the loops on your rug. Don't worry about the color because the cording will be completely covered when the rug is finished.

## Supplies

- Bent-tip needle
- Button & carpet (heavy-duty) thread
- Cotton or synthetic cording, 4" to 6" longer than the rug's perimeter (see "The Skinny on Cording" on the left)
- Hand-sewing needle
- Sewing machine or serger (optional)
- Tapestry needle
- Tapestry yarn*

*\* Count on using about a foot of tapestry yarn for every 1" of the rug's perimeter.*

**1**   After you have hooked and blocked your rug, sew 2 rows of zigzag or straight stitching about 3/4" to 1" from the outermost hooked edges. The distance between the last row of hooking and the stitching depends on the cording width. After cutting off the excess backing outside the stitching, you need to have enough backing to curl around the cording—no more. Test by wrapping around the cording. Cut away the excess backing. (Or serge the backing with a row of 3-thread overlock stitching, letting the machine cut off the excess as you stitch.) With the rug right side up, place the start of the cording on top of the excess backing. Shift the cording so that it's against the last row of hooking and not near a corner.

**2**   Roll the excess backing over the cording. Using a tapestry needle and doubled strand of heavy-duty thread, sew the backing around the cording. I like using an overcast stitch, placing the stitches about 1/4" apart. With every stitch, make sure that the needle is inserted through the backing. Continue stitching around the entire rug in this manner. Before making the final stitches, cut the end of the cording so it butts against the start of the cording. You don't need to sew the ends together.

**3**   Thread 2 strands of tapestry yarn on a bent-tip needle. I like to work with strands that are 36" long. Don't double the yarn. Place the last 1" of the threaded tapestry yarn on top of the backing, near the last row of hooking. This is your starting point, so don't position the needle near a corner and, preferably, not in the same place that you started the step 1 basting. Insert the needle through the backing from front to back, as close as possible to the last row of hooking. Pull through all but the last 1" of the yarn (the tail).

**4** Bring the needle to the front of the rug and, again, insert it through the backing. Place the needle as close as possible to the last row of hooking, next to the previous stitch. Don't sew through the cording. Pull the needle and yarn through the backing. Make sure that the yarn tail is trapped underneath the tapestry yarn that you just "whipped" over the backing. Continue making stitches in this manner. Keep the tension even, and make the stitches closer together—or farther apart—so that the backing is evenly covered. When only 3" of yarn remain on the needle, bury the yarn by pulling the needle through the previous stitches, and then cut off the yarn end. Start a new strand by stitching over the yarn tail, as already explained.

**5** Whipstitch up to the corner, making every stitch almost perpendicular to the rug's backing. At the corner, you need to make several stitches to cover the backing. Bring the needle to the front of the rug in the usual manner.

**6** Now you're going to cross over the previous stitching. Insert the needle into the same position (hole in the backing) as the previous stitch. This makes a diagonal stitch. You'll have to eyeball the depth of the new diagonal stitching line so that you can make several more stitches into the same hole. The goal is to cover the entire corner. Tension is very important at this point because you don't want the corner point to curl. Don't pull the yarn too tightly.

**7** After completing the corner, continue whipstitching along the next edge. When all of the rug's edges are covered with whipstitches, bury and cut off the yarn as explained in step 4.

**Velcro**—or any other brand of hook-and-loop tape—offers a neat alternative for hanging a rug. These tips tell you how to apply and hang a rug with hook-and-loop tape.

## Hooked on Loops

**1.** Measure the rug width from the inner edge of the rug finish. Cut both sides of 1 $1/4$"-wide hook-and-loop tape $1/2$" shorter than the rug measurement.

**2.** Pull apart the hook and loop sides. Pin the loop side, which is softer, to the wrong side of the rug so that it's directly underneath the edge finish. Center the strip across the width. Using all-purpose sewing thread, overcast stitch all of the edges to the rug.

**3.** Glue the remaining side of the tape to the right side of the dowel or hanger.

**4.** To hang the rug, press together both sides of the tape.

# Crocheted Edging

A crocheted edging is little more than rows of a very basic stitch, called a single crochet, placed evenly along the edge of a rug. Like the Flat Wool Binding (see page 18), the crocheted edging reduces wear and tear along the rug's perimeter. Worked in strips from the background wool, the finished effect beautifully complements the effect of a primitive rug.

Proving its versatility, several rows of single crochet can be a stepping-stone to an elegant effect. Janet Williams used crochet thread to work two rows of single crochet stitches along the edges of her *Corinthian Prayer Rug*, which was designed by Jane McGown Flynn. Only then did Janet add fringe, using a 3.25 mm (American D/3) crochet hook and a medium-weight crochet thread.

I'd be a bit nervous about crocheting an edging to burlap, but other backings aren't a problem.

## Supplies

- Carpet needle
- Crochet hook suitable for the yarn weight or wool strip cut
- Crochet thread or long wool strips*

*A very narrow wool strip might be easier to crochet, but you may not like the finished effect. Make sure that the width that you use fully covers the edge when it's stitched.*

## ▶ TIP  Fabric Savvy

A good choice for crocheted wool strips is the same wool that you used for your background. That said, there are times when you should seek out different options. For example, textured wool has a tendency to fray, so it wouldn't be my first choice for crocheting. Solid wool strips will make the process more enjoyable.

**1** Finish the rug with a self binding, leaving about $1/4$" of the excess backing exposed at the rug's edges. For the self binding, the backing should be folded to the rug's underside twice, which is the usual process. See pages 12 through 14 for complete instructions.

**2** Start at the middle of one side of the rug. With the rug right side up, place the tip of your hook next to the last row of loops, on top of the backing that's visible at the edge. Insert your hook from front to back through both layers of the folded backing. Leaving a 3" tail, wrap the yarn over the hook, and then pull the yarn through the backing to the top (right side) of the rug.

**3** Move the hook slightly to the left. Pull another loop of the working strip or thread through the edge of the backing and to the right side of the rug. There are now two loops on the hook. Without inserting the hook through the backing, wrap the wool strip or crochet thread around the hook. Wrap with the working strand, not the 3" tail. Pull this new loop through the two that are already on the hook. You have made a single crochet stitch.

**4** Repeat step 3 to make a line (row) of single crochet stitches along the rug's edge to the first corner. The stitches should be evenly spaced and completely cover the $1/4$" of exposed excess backing. Continue stitching around the rug. When you're back at the starting point, cut the working strip or thread 3" from the last stitch you made. Pull the cut strip or thread through the loop on the hook, take the loop off the hook, and tug on the strip or thread to secure your stitching. Use a carpet needle to pull the 3" end through the underside of the crochet stitches. Hide any remaining 3" ends in the same manner.

## Hide and Seek

If you can see the backing through the stitches, switch to a wider cut wool strip, or place the single crochet stitches closer together. If the edge is wavy, the stitches are too close together, or you need a narrower cut.

At a corner, you might need to work three single crochet stitches in the same hole so that the point won't curl up.

Chances are very slim that you'll be able to work around the entire rug with a single wool strip.

**1.** When you have only 3" of yarn remaining, stop working with it.

**2.** Start your next single crochet by inserting the hook through the backing and pull through the start of a new strip.

**3.** Place one of the 3" ends on the underside of the folded backing, parallel to the rug edge. For the time being, ignore the second end. Placing both on the backing will make a lump.

**4.** Wrap the yarn over the hook and complete the stitch in the usual manner.

**5.** Continue working additional strips while trapping the rest of the strand inside the stitches.

**6.** After finishing the edging, use a needle or the hook to pull the remaining 3" ends through the underside of the crochet stitches.

# Knitted Edging

This type of edging has been around for a long time. Mind you, these days it isn't that common on rugs.

A knitted edging is most suitable for a primitive rug. The wool strips enhance the rustic theme, as well as continue the colors selected for the rug's background and pattern. Hooker Marion Michel used the knitted edging in exactly this manner on her *Moose* rug, a pattern created by Joan Moshimer.

I wouldn't hesitate to add a knitted edging to any backing or suitably themed rug. The knitting acts as a bumper, protecting the edge of the rug from wear and tear.

Don't worry if you haven't knitted before. The following step-by-step instructions explain the entire process. If you're still struggling, just look in a knitting book, as working with wool strips is no different than knitting with yarn.

## ▶TIP Size Matters

The needle size that you select will determine whether your border is firm or soft. Larger needles are easier to work with and yield looser stitches. But this also means you'll end up with a softer border that might not wear well. It's also a good idea to experiment with wool strips of varying widths.

The samples for the step-by-step photos on pages 34 through 36 were made with 5 mm (American size 8) knitting needles and 1/4"-wide, crosswise, wool strips. Marion knit the border for her *Moose* rug with 3/8"-wide strips on 6 mm (American size 10) needles. If you want, you can cut strips double the desired width and fold them in half lengthwise when knitting.

## Supplies

- Bent-tip needle
- Carpet needle
- Knitting needles (see "Size Matters" on the right)
- Button & carpet (heavy-duty) or all-purpose sewing thread
- Rotary cutter, clear ruler, and self-healing cutting mat (optional)
- Safety pins (optional)
- Wool strips, 1/4" to 3/8" wide (see "Size Matters")

Edge B

Edge A

**1**

**1** Finish the rug as desired. A cotton binding or self binding are both suitable. (See pages 12 through 17.) Cut your wool strips to the desired width. (See "Size Matters" on page 33.) You can make a long, continuous wool strip with a clear ruler, rotary cutter, and self-healing mat. Remove the selvage. Working along the width of the wool, cut a strip to your desired width. Don't cut through the far edge (Edge B). Instead, cut to within $3/8$" of the edge. Shift the ruler the desired strip width and cut through Edge B and across the fabric width, stopping $3/8$" from Edge A. Continue cutting strips, alternating the edge that you cut through.

Insert needle here

**2**

**2** Before you start making stitches, you must secure a loop on your hook. Start by making a loop near the end of the wool strip. Reach through the loop, and pull through a loop of the wool strip. Slide this new loop on to one of the knitting needles. Pull both ends of the strip until the strip is snug. Make sure the knot is loose enough to slide easily on the needle.

**3**

**3** There are several ways to make more stitches on a knitting needle. The simplest is explained here, but you can find other options in most knitting reference books. Wrap the longer (working) end of the wool strip around your thumb from left to right. This positions the shorter end of the strip, which is closest to the needle, on top, so that the loop is "locked." Place the needle in the palm of your hand, and slide the needle through the loop. Use the needle to lift the loop off the thumb. You now have two loops on the needle. Continue adding loops until you have enough for the desired width of the border.

**4** When you have enough stitches on the needle, you're ready to knit the first row. Insert the second needle through the uppermost loop, from bottom to top. Wrap the working strip around the tip of the second needle, from left to right. Pull this new loop through the old loop. Lift the old loop off the first needle. You now have 1 loop on the right (second) needle. The first (left) needle has 1 less loop. In other words, if you started with 10 loops, you now have 9 on the left needle. Repeat this step until no loops remain on the left needle. One row is complete. Place the right needle in the left hand and knit the second row in the same manner. All rows should have the same number of stitches.

**5** Continue making rows until the border is long enough for one side of the rug. When you're about 3" from the end of the wool strip, leave the end on the underside of the border and make the next loop with the start of a new strip. Don't stop short of the corner. With the right side of the knitting facing you, knit all but the last 2 stitches. In other words, if you cast on 10 stitches, there are now 8 on the right needle and 2 on the left. Switch the needles so that the right needle is now in the left hand. Ignoring the 2 unworked stitches that are now on the right needle, knit all of the stitches on the needle in your left hand. You have just made 2 short rows. Note: The photos for steps 4, 5, and 6 show the corner worked in a contrasting wool strip so that you can see the short rows. Use the same wool for the sides and corners on your border.

**6** Repeat step 4, but stop the row when 4 stitches remain on the left needle. Make the next row in the usual manner (turn the work by switching the needles to the opposite hands). You have now made 2 more rows, worked on 6 stitches. Make another set of rows on 4 stitches, and then a final set of rows on 2 stitches. Half of your wedge-shaped corner is complete.

**7** Now you reverse the process, knitting 4 stitches on the next 2 rows, 6 on the next 2 rows, and so on until you have knitted 2 rows that both have 10 stitches. Make the next side of the rug by working all of the stitches on every row. Continue making sides and corners in the same manner.

**8** You're ready to end the knitting after making the fourth corner. At the start of the next row, knit the first 2 stitches. Using the tip of the left needle, lift the first stitch on the right needle over the second. You now have 1 stitch on the right needle. Knit another stitch on the left needle. You now have 2 stitches on the right needle. Again, lift the first stitch on the right needle over the second.

**9** Repeat step 6 until you've knitted all of the stitches off the left needle and have 1 stitch remaining on the right needle. Cut the working wool strip about 10" from the needles, lift the last loop off the right needle, and pull the cut end through the loop. This knots the last stitch.

**10** With the right side up, butt the last and first rows together. Thread the end of the strip through the eye of a carpet needle. Pull the needle and strip through the first stitch of the first row. Now pull it through the first stitch of the last row. Move up 1 stitch and pull the strip through the second stitch of the first, and then last, rows. When all of stitches are woven together, weave the strip through the underside of the border and cut if off.

**11** Butt the inner edge of the border against the edge of the rug. If desired, use safety pins to temporarily hold the border against the rug edge. Pull the bent-tip needle and a doubled length of heavy-duty thread through a strand of the backing, at the edge of the rug. Now pull the needle and thread through a stitch at the edge of the knitted edging. Continue sewing all of the sides together. On the underside there will be loose ends wherever you started a new wool strip. Weave these ends into the underside.

## Corner Summary

| | |
|---|---|
| **Row 1 (right side facing):** Knit 8 stitches, turn. | **Row 9 (right side):** Knit 4 stitches, turn. |
| **Row 2 (wrong side facing):** Knit 8 stitches, turn. | **Row 10:** Knit 4 stitches, turn. |
| **Row 3:** Knit 6 stitches, turn. | **Row 11:** Knit 6 stitches, turn. |
| **Row 4:** Knit 6 stitches, turn. | **Row 12:** Knit 6 stitches, turn. |
| **Row 5:** Knit 4 stitches, turn. | **Row 13:** Knit 8 stitches, turn. |
| **Row 6:** Knit 4 stitches, turn. | **Row 14:** Knit 8 stitches, turn. |
| **Row 7:** Knit 2 stitches, turn. | **Row 15:** Knit 10 stitches, turn. |
| **Row 8:** Knit 2 stitches, turn. | **Row 16:** Knit 10 stitches, turn. |

## ▶TIP Lowdown on the Countdown

The sample shown in the step-by-step photos was made with $1/4$"-wide strips. Ten stitches yielded a 3"-wide border. The height of the stitches when stacked on the needle does not represent the finished width of the knitting. If your wool is thick or you're using a different strip width, you may need to experiment with the number of stitches to achieve a pleasing width. Make a best guess at the number of stitches, and then knit a few rows according to the following steps. If you don't like the width, start over.

# CHAPTER FOUR

The binding has been added, an edging is in place . . . what more can your rug possibly need? At this point, it isn't so much what the rug needs as what would further personalize and enhance it. Add a label. Apply fringe. Consider one of several ways to hang the piece on a wall. There's so much you can do.

Often, instructions about finishing will tell you to add a label or fringe without explaining how. Sure, you can muddle through this on your own, but I want to ease the process. Along the way, I can offer you very specific information and guidance so that you won't repeat the mistakes I made as a beginner.

# Expanding Your Horizons

## Fringed Edges

We've all admired the beautiful fringe on Oriental carpets, but did you know it looks great on other types of rugs? I've always felt that you can put any edging on any rug. It's a matter of personal choice.

The only thing that should limit you are technical considerations, like the backing suitability or something on the rug that will hinder the application of the edging.

Fringe, for example, isn't suitable for a rug that's finished with a self binding. The backing will show. My *Magic Carpet* rug, designed by Patsy Becker, shows fringe applied to corded and whipped edges.

This proves that although fringe is often added after applying a crocheted edging, a row of single crochet stitches isn't necessary.

▶TIP **Long and Short on Length**

These instructions create a 6"-long fringe, but yours can be any length. Merely cut the cardboard 3" wide and the same length as the desired fringe. For example, if you want 8" fringe on the rug, then cut your cardboard rectangle 3" x 8".

**1** Complete the rug edge with a corded and whipped edging or self binding. If desired, add a crocheted edging. Set aside the rug until step 2. Wrap yarn around the lengthwise edges of the cardboard until it's completely covered. You want all of the strands to be the same 6" length, so don't overlap the wraps. Cut through all of the strands along one lengthwise edge. You now have 12" yarn strands (twice as long as the desired finished fringe length).

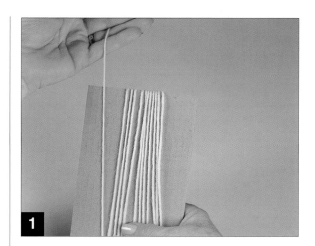

**2** Start near the corner at one narrow end of the rug. Insert the crochet hook through the front to the back. If you whipped the rug edges, the crochet hook is inserted at the inner edge of the whipping. On a crocheted edging, insert the hook through the center of the stitch. Fold a yarn strand in half. Place the fold (the mid-point) in the crochet hook's bowl. Pull the yarn loop to the front of the work. You only need a few inches. Insert the crochet hook in the same position and pull through as many strands as you want to knot together.

**3** Holding all of the strands together pull the ends through the loops on the right. Snug the knot against the edge of the rug. For the next fringe bundle, again insert the crochet hook through the rug a short distance from the first bundle. Pull several strands through this new position and knot them together. Continue making fringe along the row in the same manner.

▶**TIP** Less Is More

In a medium-weight yarn, pulling 3 strands through 1 hole gives you a nice 6-strand knotted fringe. Using more strands makes the fringe too bulky. Depending on the characteristics of your yarn, you might like more—or fewer—strands in each position.

# Creative Labels

It's important to label your rugs. The label will help it return home if it's lost, identify it if it's in a show, increase its value, and preserve information for future generations of your family.

You might find that you enjoy the process of labeling your work. Like a painter signing a canvas, this little flourish could draw upon your sense of accomplishment and bring closure to your project. If I've been working for a long time on a large rug, I can hardly wait to apply the label. As the finishing gets closer and closer to completion, my anticipation mounts.

With so many ways to sign your rug, there's no excuse for ignoring this final step. You can hook your name into the rug, or attach a label. I like the label on Janet Williams' *Corinthian Prayer* (the bottom rug in the photo.) She included a provenance, which is additional information about the rug and the creation process. The provenance can include the reason for making the rug, the dye colors, and dyeing techniques.

The type and size of the label will limit what you can include. I like a complete record, so my labels often include the name of the pattern and the designer, my name (or initials), and the completion date. Some hookers will put the starting, rather than completion, date on their label.

People who are just learning to hook might include the name of the teacher who offered creative guidance and technical advice. If it's a commemorative rug, you might even want to include details about the event.

After creating your label, simply slipstitch it to the back of your rug. If the fabric edges might fray, turn them under or else pink them. Make sure you don't pull out any loops as you attach the label.

The following list explains some of the label options to consider.

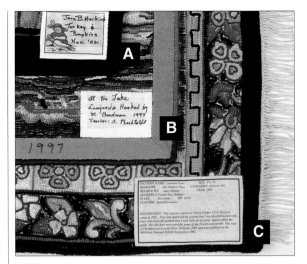

**A**    Several companies sell labels suitable for handwriting. I like to buy my labels. When you're recording details on the fabric, make sure you use an indelible ink pen. I use a Sharpie Industrial, a fine-point permanent marker by Sanford. Other brands will work, as long as they're intended for use as laundry marking pens. Most manufactured labels are cotton with pinked edges. The motif on the label of Joan Harkin's rug (designed by Fredericksburg Rugs) is a cute touch.

**B**    There's nothing wrong with a low-tech approach. Merely cut a 5" cotton square, and then use an indelible ink pen to write the details. Peg Boudreau used a Magic Marker to write on the bleached muslin label for her original design.

**C**    With access to a computer, you can make personalized labels by running specialty fabric through your printer. Most office supply and fabric stores carry the product. If your writing isn't tidy, this is a great option. You can also include considerably more information because the type will be clearer.

Janet Williams made the computer label that's stitched to the bottom rug in the photo. She hooked *Corinthian Prayer*, which was designed by Jane McGown Flynn.

**D** You also could stitch your name and completion date on the fabric if you have a sewing machine that can embroider letters. When Susan Feller finished hooking *Lauren*, which she also designed, she used a machine-embroidered label.

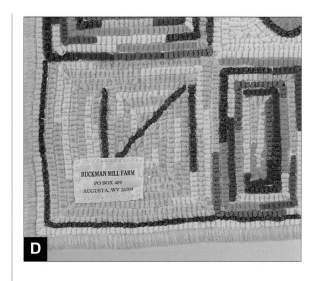

RUCKMAN MILL FARM
PO BOX 409
AUGUSTA, WV 26704

**D**

**E** You may have seen initials and a completion date hooked into the corner of a rug. This is a nice permanent record of the work and a good alternative to stitching a label to the underside. Plan the position and size of your "signature." It should be proportional to the rug's dimensions. A logo that includes a signature is usually about 3" tall. Using a permanent pen, sketch your initials, the year, or your logo on the backing. If your sketching isn't the greatest, why not use a stencil to draw your initials on the backing?

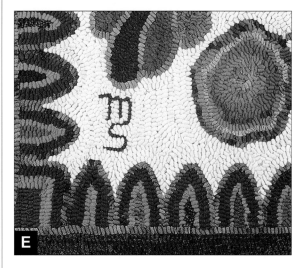

**E**

### Why Knot?

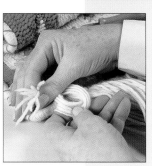

Strands of fringe can also be joined easily with an overhand knot. This photo shows the fringe in a contrasting color so it's easier for you to see the effect.

## Carpet Tack Strips Wall Mount

Long before I developed the confidence to frame my pieces, my husband, Dick, was mounting my rugs with carpet tack strips. This is a simple process that needs very little equipment. It's also a great way to hang a rug without stitching anything to the back of it. The photo of my Lib Callaway *Wedding Rug,* above, was taken with it hanging. As you can see, none of the hardware is visible when the piece is in position on the wall.

Whatever backing or finish your rug features, this hanging method is suitable. Carpet tacks won't damage burlap, as long as care is taken when hanging the rug. I've only hung rugs that were finished with self binding or whipped edges. But this hanging method is suitable for any backing or finish.

### Supplies

- Carpet tack strips* (see step 1)
- 1/4"-thick fiber board, peg board or plywood, the same width and length as the rug
- Hammer
- Nails
- Saw
- Wood screws or other picture-hanging hardware

*Used to attach wall-to-wall carpeting, these are 1"-wide wood strips that have tacks protruding along the length.*

**1** With the tacks face up, place a strip on the peg board so that the outer edge is flush with the upper edge of the board. Attach the strip to the board with nails positioned about 18" apart. Nail another strip across the bottom of the board. The rug shown on page 42 is 3' wide by 2' long, so no additional support is needed to hang it. A heavier rug needs diagonal strips, positioned as shown by the masking tape in the photo on the right.

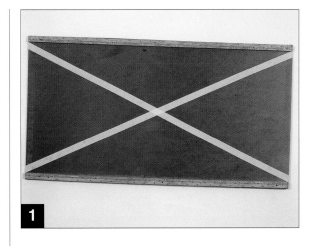

**2** Block the rug. Flip over the board and attach the picture-hanging hardware to the side that doesn't have carpet tack strips. Hang the board. (If desired, you can screw the board directly to the wall.) Press the rug on to the carpet tack strips on the board. Be careful because the tacks are very sharp. If the tacks protrude through the carpet, remove the carpet and cut off the tip of each tack.

▶**TIP** **X Marks the Spot**

You need 2—possibly 4—carpet tack strips, depending on the size of your rug. Count on cutting 2 lengths that are each the same width as the rug. If your rug is more than 48" wide, you also need 2 more carpet tack strips. Measure the rug from the upper right corner to a lower left corner. Cut 2 pieces to this length.

A rug's dimensions are limiting. The carpet tack strips won't hold a heavy rug. The largest rug that I've successfully hung is 30" x 71".

## Sleeve and Dowel Wall Hanging

Several of the rugs that are shown in this book have a fabric sleeve sewn across the upper edge. My friends and I like to hang our work, and the sleeve and dowel approach seems to be the preferred method. As you can see on the back of the rug, a sleeve is very simple. Susan Feller, who hooked and designed this rug, *Lauren*, used the sleeve and dowel method to hang it.

In order to show you the sleeve and dowel on the back of the rug, we used a wood dowel that's longer than the rug's width. Your dowel for your rug will be shorter, so it's invisible when the rug is on the wall.

A sleeve can be attached to any type of backing. When I plan to hang a rug this way, I prefer a self binding. But, as you can see on Susan's piece here and in the step-by-step photos that follow (featuring *Uncle Sam*, which Susan hooked and designed), other finishes can be used.

I wouldn't use a sleeve and dowel to hang a rug that is more than 40" wide.

### Supplies

- All-purpose sewing thread
- Hand-sewing needle
- Medium-weight muslin or single-fold bias or twill tape
- Saw
- Straight pins
- Wood dowel or painted metal rod*

*The dowel you select needs to be strong enough to support the rug's weight. If it isn't thick enough, it'll bow in the center. I use a 1/2" dowel for an 18" x 24" rug. Lauren, shown here is 20" x 24". Uncle Sam, shown on page 45, also designed and hooked by Susan Feller, is 18" x 27". Both rugs are hung on a 1/2"-diameter wood dowel.*

**1** Finish the rug as desired, and then block it. Cut the dowel $1/2$" shorter than the rug's width. Cut the muslin strip twice the desired width of the finished sleeve. The finished sleeve can be any width that's wider than the dowel. A good finished width is $2^1/2$" wide. In this case, the muslin strip is cut 5" wide. Cut the length of muslin, bias tape, or twill tape $1^1/2$" shorter than the rug's width, as measured from the inside edge of the border or edge treatment. Don't add extra length to the muslin or tape because, upon completion, both ends must stop short of the rug's lengthwise edges. If you're using bias or twill tape for the sleeve, proceed to step 2. Fold both lengthwise edges of the muslin strip so the raw edges meet in the center of the wrong side. This is the wrong side of the sleeve. Press the folds.

**2** Place the wrong side of the sleeve against the underside of the rug. Shift the sleeve so that the upper lengthwise edge is just below the edge treatment. If the edge is corded and whipped, for example, the top of the sleeve is underneath the inner edge of the whipstitches. Gently push up the bottom of the sleeve so that it's $1^1/4$" from the upper edge. Don't sew the sleeve flat against the rug. The sleeve needs to puff to accommodate the dowel's width. For a large dowel, you may need more than $1/4$" of excess backing, so pin the bottom of the sleeve closer to the upper edge. Don't be too generous because you don't want to see the top of the sleeve when the rug is hung. Using an overcast stitch, tapestry needle, and doubled strand of all-purpose thread, sew the long sides of the sleeve to the rug's underside as pinned. Slide the dowel into the sleeve, and hang your piece. If desired, cut a notch in each end of the dowel and pass a hanging cord through the notch.

▶TIP **Cleaning Up the Ends**

I prefer to leave the open ends of the sleeve raw. It's a bit difficult to insert the dowel when the short ends are finished by folding them under. If you want finished ends, cut the muslin strip, bias tape, or twill tape $1/2$" longer than the rug's width. Before sewing the sleeve to the rug, turn under $1/2$" at both of the short ends.

▶TIP **Smooth Operator**

You can perfect the appearance of your rug by making sure the bottom edges don't curl. First, make sure that the rug is blocked properly. Now sew flat washers to each of the lower corners, on the underside of the rug, to weigh down the curled edges.

# Framing a Rug

I f it hasn't already happened, there will come a point when you'll decide that the rugs you make deserve to be framed. This can be a difficult decision because framing is expensive.

It also takes a lot of courage to give a precious rug to a stranger. Not all framers have enough experience or technical skills to properly present your work. I was lucky enough to stumble across Richard Lavdanski, who works at the Rag Shop in Phillipsburg, New Jersey. I have a special place in my heart for him because he's an excellent framer, and he considers rug hooking a viable art form. Richard framed all three of my rugs in the photo (*Flying Santa* is on top, with *Angel Starduster* in the center, and *Winter Fun* on the bottom. The pattern designers, from top to bottom, are George Kahnle, Patsy Becker, and Lib Callaway.)

## Advice to Share

Richard was kind enough to give me the following advice to share with you so that your framed rug will look the best that it can.

- Don't trim the excess backing around your work. Leave at least 1". When I'm finished hooking, I merely block the piece and take it directly to Richard. I don't trim off any of the backing! It's best to leave this process to the professional, so that there's enough excess to properly mount the work.

- The color of the frame is extremely important. Don't pick a frame to match the primary color in your piece. Instead, pick the rug's secondary color for the frame.

- The best frame for rug hooking has a deep rabbet groove. The rug backing is inserted into this recessed line in the back of the frame, along each side.

- Make sure that all of the framing materials are acid free. They'll last longer and won't damage the rug fibers.

- A large rug needs the support of a heavier mounting board. Richard says it should be at least $3/8$" thick, so that it can handle the mounting staples or tacks.

- Many of the common frames suitable for pictures don't work well with hooked rugs. Make sure your framer helps you select the right product.

- If a framer suggests glass on top . . . grab your rug and run! Air should circulate around the rug so that the wool can breathe. A glass top will block this process, making the fibers deteriorate.

- Don't hang the framed rug in direct sunlight. The sun will fade the colors in the fibers.

- Round and oval frames are available but aren't as common. They're far more expensive than the rectangular ones. If you're going to hook a round or oval rug and want it framed, check with the framer to get the standard sizes. The framing costs will really escalate if the framer has to create a custom-sized frame. A round, oval, or irregular-shaped rug can be placed in a rectangular-shaped frame with a matt or a plaque to fill in the empty areas.

# CHAPTER FIVE

# A Finished Rug Gallery

Most of the step-by-step photos in this book were created with a huge, three-part rug that I have been working on for quite some time. But I also wanted you to see finishing treatments on completed rugs, so that you could enjoy a wide range of styles, treatments, and patterns.

I couldn't believe my good fortune when so many friends and students agreed to let me show you their rugs. You've already seen page after page of detail photos. Enough teasing. Now it's time to show you the entire rugs. Just to make this visual feast a banquet, I also included a few extras to inspire and motivate you.

**1** Magic Carpet, 22" x 30",
#6- and 8-cut wool on monk's cloth. Designed
by Patsy Becker. Hooked by Margaret Siano,
Flemington, New Jersey, 1991.

This rug was a gift for my daughter, Dr. Margaret
Lutz. For unity, the fringe is made with the same
yarn that I used to whip the edges. Every knotted
bundle of fringe has 12 strands. For additional
interest, I used long overcast stitches of pink
embroidery floss (three strands) on the long
edges.

**2** Caswell Fruit Basket,
71" x 30 1/2", #6- and 8-cut wool on linen.
Designed by Lib Callaway. Hooked by Margaret
Siano, Flemington, New Jersey, 1996.

I hooked this rug in 1996 to test my ability to
portray fruit. I modified the border with lamb-
tongue shapes. By eliminating the banner that
was in the original design, the fruit basket takes
center stage. I was so happy with the outcome
that I had it framed by Richard Lavdanski, who
works at the Rag Shop in Phillipsburg, New
Jersey. Now the piece hangs triumphantly in the
family room.

**3** Winter Fun, 68" x 33", #6- and 8-
cut wool on burlap. Designed by Lib Callaway.
Hooked by Margaret Siano, Flemington, New
Jersey, 1997.

This pattern sat for more than 10 years after I
started it. After attending a workshop on pictorial
rugs, I finally picked it up again. The workshop
was a pivotal event in my hooking because I now
prefer making pictorial rugs. They keep my
interest because I can depict my children and
grandchildren, pets, homes, and other important
things and events in the pattern.

**1. Magic Carpet**

**2. Caswell Fruit Basket**

**3. Winter Fun**

**4** **Corinthian Prayer**, 58" x 37", #3-, 4-, and 5-cut wool on linen. Designed by Jane McGown Flynn. Hooked by Janet Williams, Skillman, New Jersey, 2002.

I received a special gift in 2002: a loaned rug that symbolizes a friend's trust. Janet Williams hooked this rug as a Christmas gift for her son. As all the photos for *The Secrets of Finishing Hooked Rugs* were taken in December, I needed to take the rug to the studio before Christmas. Making this book was something new for me, so I didn't know how long I'd need to keep the rug. I did get it back to her in time. Janet's technique, sense of color, and balance are impeccable.

**5** **Just Settin'**, 16" x 16", #3- and 4-cut wool on rug warp. Designed by Jane McGown Flynn. Hooked by Peg Boudreau, Branchburg, New Jersey, 2002.

I like the way this piece is mounted on cotton-covered Masonite. After completing the hooking, Peg Boudreau pulled the excess backing to the underside of the Masonite and sewed the edges together. The backing shows along the edges because it blends with the hooked straw. This work was entered in the McGown Biennial Exhibition in October 2002.

**6** **At The Lake**, 42" x 24", #3- and 4-cut wool on rug warp. Designed and hooked by Peg Boudreau, Branchburg, New Jersey, 1997.

I especially admire the whipped and corded edging on this rug. As Peg Boudreau worked around the edge, she matched the tapestry's yarn color to the closest loop colors. (There's a detail photo on page 26.) The treatment along the birch tree is exceptional. The rug depicts the lake near Peg's summer home, with her children manning the boats. She attached a $1^1/4$" wide twill tape sleeve to the back so that the rug can hang from a wooden dowel.

**5. Just Settin'**

**6. At The Lake**

51

**7** **Poor Kitty,** 22" x 36", #6-, 7-, 8-, and 9-cut wool on monk's cloth. Designed and hooked by Laurie Rubinetti, Milford, New Jersey, 2001.

This whimsical pattern is an original. Laurie Rubinetti created and hooked it, then enhanced the pattern by adding a single row of braid. Laurie's colors choices were inspired by her love of zinnias. The vibrant colors contribute to the sense of energy and activity that's in this piece. The work, which has a monk's cloth backing, is finished with a self binding and a sleeve so that she can use a wood dowel to hang it from the back of a door.

**8** **Flower and Flame,** 36" x 36", #6-, 7-, 8-, and 9-cut wool on burlap. Designed by Lib Callaway. Hooked by Laurie Rubinetti, Milford, New Jersey, 2000.

This is one of Lib Callaway's most beautiful patterns. As you would expect, it has been hooked many, many times. To expertly finish her colorful version, Laurie Rubinetti applied three rows of braid. She purchased extra wool yardage so that she could make the braid with the same material that's in the rug. Carrying colors from the hooking into the edging is a nice way to link diverse elements.

**9** **Moose,** 28" x 20", #6- and 8-cut wool on burlap. Designed by Joan Moshimer. Hooked by Marion Michel, Lambertville, New Jersey, 2000.

A knitted edging made with the rug wool showcases this simple pattern. Marion Michel finished the edges of her rug with a 2"-wide cotton binding. She didn't turn the entire width of the binding to the underside. Instead, 1" extends straight out from the rug. The knitted edging is sewn on top of this lip.

**8. Flower and Flame**

**9. Moose**

**11. Snowman and Christmas Tree**

**12** **Angel Starduster,** 37" x 25", #8-cut wool on monk's cloth. Designed by Patsy Becker. Hooked by Margaret Siano, Flemington, New Jersey, 1998.

I love the pattern, but I wanted to jazz up the background and stars. Spot dyeing was the obvious solution. Before cutting the wool strips, I randomly applied dye to the background yardage. When placing the pattern on the backing, I made sure that there would be plenty of excess backing around the edges so that the framer would find it easier to mount.

**10. Uncle Sam**

**10** **Uncle Sam,** 18" x 27", #8-cut wool on monk's cloth. Designed and hooked by Susan Feller, Augusta, West Virginia, 2002.

This is a very patriotic rug, very much in tune with today's times. Notice that Susan Feller hooked initials and the completion date into the lower corners? I can't stress enough how important it is to sign your rug. You don't have to hook anything into the rug. Simply sewing a label to the underside will do the trick. Future generations are sure to appreciate the information. Remember that the life of a hooked rug can exceed a hundred years and span three generations.

**11** **Snowman and Christmas Tree,** 2" x 3" each, #3-cut wool on burlap. Designed and hooked by Barbara Lugg, Frenchtown, New Jersey, 2002.

What a fun way to get in the mood for Christmas! Barbara's finishing touches add so much character to the pieces: A small piece of wool is wrapped around the snowman's neck and the Christmas tree is covered with bead "ornaments." The pins were completed with wool that was pinked around the edges, and then glued to the backing.

**13** **Happy Time Bears,** 36" x 24", #6-cut wool on linen. Designed by Jane McGown Flynn (The House of Price). Hooked by Cathy Edwards, Phillipsburg, New Jersey, 2001

Doesn't this pattern take you back to your childhood? Cathy brought the images to life by sculpting the bumblebee and the bears' noses. Tuffs of lamb's-wool are hooked into the bears' ears. The rug is finished with a flat wool binding.

**12. Angel Starduster**

**13. Happy TIme Bears**

*55*

## 14. Turkey and Pumpkins

### 16. Bellsnickles

**15** **Flying Santa,** 32" x 18",
#8-cut wool on monk's cloth. Designed by
George Kahnle. Hooked by Margaret Siano,
Flemington, New Jersey, 2000.

This whimsical pattern was a happy one for me
to hook. I made it at a workshop hosted by a
very funny man, Dick LaBarge. Several of my
best friends were there so we had a great time.
I used sheep's fleece to hook the beard.
Hooking this material is less demanding
because the sizes of the loops aren't as
important. In fact, I taught myself to hook it.

**16** **Bellsnickles,** 13$\frac{1}{2}$" x 4$\frac{1}{2}$",
#8-cut wool on burlap. Designed  by Sharon
Ballard. (The green Bellsnickle was hooked
by Margaret Siano, Flemington, New Jersey,
1996; the brown Bellsnickle was hooked by
Sharon Ballard, Lebanon, New Jersey, 1990.)

## 15. Flying Santa

**14** **Turkey and Pumpkins,**
24" x 18", #7-cut wool on monk's cloth.
Designed by Laurice Heath. Hooked
by Joan Harkins, Holland, Pennsylvania,
2002.

This is a very nice seasonal rug because it
uses beautiful, warm autumn colors. I would
show this rug to any class of beginner rug
hookers that wanted to learn more about
finishing. The edges are completed with a
cotton binding that has mitered corners
(there's a detail of the back in a photo on
page 17). The whipped edges are well done.
And the hooker, Joan Harkins, even added an
attractive label.

For Christmas one year, Sharon Ballard gave
me the smallest of these two delightful
"Bellsnickles." I loved the gift so much that I
decided to hook a second. After hooking,
Sharon sewed together the edges and then
stuffed the shape with a polyfiber filling.

# CHAPTER SIX

*Some stitches and techniques are the foundation of many of the finishing procedures explained in* **The Secrets of Finishing Hooked Rugs.** *Rather than repeating them with every technique, they are grouped here, for easy reference. This is not a definitive primer, nor are these instructions presented to imply that there's only one right way to execute them. As you develop your skills, you'll decide what's best for you.*

# The Finishing Primer

## Essential Stitches

I'd be hard pressed to find a completed hand-hooked rug that didn't have at least some hand stitching somewhere on it. To complete a piece, you'll need to use a blindstitch, overcast stitch, running stitch, or whipstitch. You may not need all four of these stitches, however. I suspect that you'll find one most comfortable to make, and use it for almost everything. When sewing the loose edge of a binding to the backside of a rug, for example, you can use a whipstitch or an invisible blindstitch.

Here are instructions for these simple stitches. At the end of this section, you'll also find instructions to join wool strips or binding with a diagonal seam.

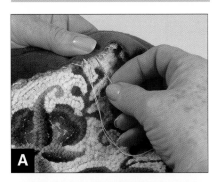

### A Blindstitch

1. Roll back the first 1/4" of the upper edge. Working on the exposed underside of this rolled edge, make a small stitch horizontal to the edge.
2. Shift the needle to the fabric that's the lower layer. Make a small stitch in the lower layer, slightly ahead of the previous stitch. The thread between the two stitches is diagonal.
3. Move forward a bit and make another small stitch in the exposed underside of the upper fabric layer.
4. Continue alternating stitches between the fabric layers until the edges are joined for the desired length. Roll the upper layer back to its final position.

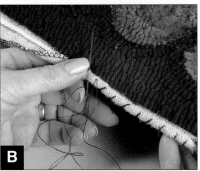

### B Overcast Stitch

1. Diagonally insert the needle through the lower layer and out the upper layer.
2. Pull the needle through both fabric layers and repeat step 1.
3. Continue making diagonal stitches until the edges are joined for the desired length.

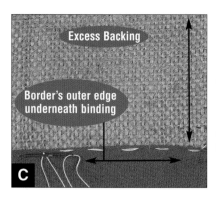

Excess Backing

Border's outer edge underneath binding

**C**

##  

**C** Running Stitch

1. Insert the needle from front to back through both fabric layers.
2. Pull the needle out of the fabric a short distance beyond—and in a straight line with—the insertion point.
3. Continue inserting the needle in and out of the fabric layers in a straight line until the edges are joined for the desired length.

**D** Whipstitch

1. Insert the needle, perpendicular to the fabric edge, through the fabric from front to back.
2. Pull the needle through both fabric layers and repeat step 1.
3. Continue making stitches perpendicular to the fabric edge for the desired length.

**E** Making a Diagonal Seam

1. Place a wool strip horizontally on a table, right side up. Place the second strip, right side down, on top of—and perpendicular to—the first.
2. Sew the ends together with a diagonal, medium-length straight stitch that starts at the upper left corner of the top strip and ends at the lower right corner of the strip underneath.

### Stitch Basics

Whatever stitch you choose, all have certain elements in common.

- You can stitch with a single strand of thread, but a doubled length has more strength.
- Before making the first stitch, simply knot the ends together so that the stitching will be secure.
- When stitching on the underside of a rug, you might want to dig the needle into the backing. The needle should grab enough of the rug wool for secure stitching.
- Using a 36" length of thread will give you enough to work with, but won't be unwieldy.
- Use button & carpet (heavy-duty) thread, color-matched to the binding, for extra-strong stitches.

It's best not to move the rug until it's completely dry. Rugs take up a lot of space, and I have a busy household, so I do all of my blocking on the kitchen counter in the evening. There's less activity at this time. Everyone in the family knows they aren't supposed to touch my pieces. I'm an early riser, so the next morning I pick up my rug before the hungry hordes amass for breakfast.

## *Blocking*

Just as your clothes need a good pressing to look their best, your rug needs to be set with heat and steam. Blocking helps the loops look less like individual pieces, and ensures that the sides of the finished rug are the shape that you intended. Although blocking can't always force a substantially warped rug into shape, it can straighten edges and smooth curves.

Blocking isn't a once-and-done process. You'll need to block a rug after the hooking is finished and you're ready to start the finishing. You may also need to block a rug again, after the finishing is completed.

### Supplies

- 2 bath towels, one larger than the rug
- Flat, hard surface larger than the rug
- Iron

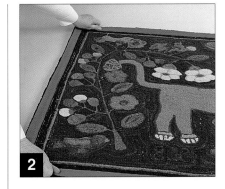

**1** If you're blocking the rug before finishing, trim off the excess backing.

**2** As you hook, you have to make sure that the edges of your rug are straight. But if they look a bit wobbly when the hooking is complete, there is a solution. Grasp opposite corners and tug to straighten the sides. If the edges are still troublesome, see "Straight and Narrow" on page 60.

**3** Place a bath towel on the blocking surface. Put your rug, wrong side up, on top of the towel. Wet the remaining towel, wring it out, and place it on top of the rug.

**4** Set the iron for a medium to high heat. Place the iron in the center of the rug, on top of the upper towel. Let it rest in position for a few seconds. Your iron heat is set correctly if the towel steams. Lift the iron and move it over a few inches. Again let it sit on the towel for a few seconds. Continue in this manner until the iron has rested over the entire surface.

**5** Remove the top towel. Turn the rug right side up. Again place the towel on top of the rug. Repeat step 4. Let the rug dry naturally.

# Care and Cleaning

Finishing a rug involves a lot of handling, so there's a good chance that the rug might need cleaning. This doesn't have to be a grand effort. For everyday cleaning I simply go over my rugs with a small hand-held vacuum (like a Dust Buster) or use my central vacuum system. Upright and canister vacuums will also work, as long as you don't use a beater bar. The circulating bar can grab hold of the loops hooked into the rug and pull them out. I vacuum my rugs as frequently as once a week if they're in a high-traffic area.

For a more thorough cleaning job, you can opt for soap suds, chemical cleaners, snow, or a professional rug cleaner. Be cautious with dry cleaners, unless you are familiar with your dry cleaner and are sure he knows exactly what he's doing. Whatever method you choose, remember to take extra care with a rug that's hooked on burlap because this fiber is more fragile than other backings. Since burlap doesn't age well, I avoid sharply bending a rug hooked on burlap when handling it.

Whatever the backing on your rug, the best care you can give it is to keep it out of high traffic areas. Puppies and cats with claws can destroy a work of art faster than you can imagine.

That said, your rug is meant to be enjoyed as much as possible. If this means putting it on a floor . . . do it. If it means hanging the rug as you would a painting . . . do it!

## Straight and Narrow

Is there a bulge in your rug? This was caused by hooking the rug too tightly, which is called packing. To fix the problem, it's time to vent some steam. I learned a neat trick from an 86-year-old hooker. It's so effective that I've yet to encounter a student's rug I haven't been able to flatten. This simple process seems to relax the fibers, so the next day it's easier to flatten the rug by blocking.

**1.** Place the rug face down on a damp towel.

**2.** Roll the rug in the towel and let it rest like this overnight.

**3.** Unroll the rug and block it.

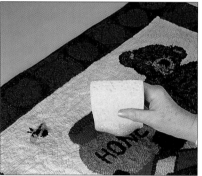

**Soap Suds**—I clean this way whenever a rug begins to look dull and dingy. Put a bit of water in a bucket and pour in some dishwashing detergent. I like Dawn because it has lots of suds. Whip the water with your hand to create some froth. Dip the sponge into the suds. Don't put the sponge into the water. Gently rub the suds over the rug's surface. Don't saturate the rug. The suds should rest on the rug surface for just a few seconds. They don't sink in. To complete the cleaning, place the rug flat in a ventilated area to dry before returning it to its home.

**Chemical Cleaners**—With one exception, I don't use these products. When one of my rugs has a spot that won't come out, I count on Carbona because it doesn't remove color. It's sold in most supermarkets. There's a sponge on top of the bottle, so all you have to do is tip it and rub it on the rug. Let the rug air dry before putting it back on the floor.

**Snow**—Sometimes the most old-fashioned methods are the best. This cleaning method is a good example. After a dry, powdery snowfall, take your rug outside. Place it right side down on the snow. Sprinkle a bit of snow over the rug and gently brush back and forth with a broom.

You'll be amazed at the amount of dirt left behind on the snow when you pick up the rug. The rug colors will also be brighter. I don't know why this happens. . . it's just a little miracle.

Take the rug into the house, and let it dry naturally on the floor.

**Professional Cleaning**—Some hookers get their pieces dry-cleaned or take them to a rug cleaner. I've never done this, but I know women who have. A few have had their rugs completely ruined. The right cleaner will do a great job, so get recommendations before you trust your piece to anyone. Better yet, look for a pro that advertises rug cleaning.

A few years ago I watched a specialist clean a rug that was worth $15,000. His crew laid the rug in a driveway and hosed it down with a special solution. What an eye-opener!

## Cleaning Don'ts

- Never use the vacuum's beater bar. This powerful tool will pull out the loops.
- Hide the power brush.
- Never shake or beat a rug. Such a violent action breaks the fibers in the backing. Burlap is especially susceptible to damage.
- If you need to store a rug, roll it with the right side facing out. Never wrap it in plastic. Plastic prevents the rug from breathing. Most hookers roll our rugs right side out, wrap them in an old sheet, and put them under a bed for safekeeping.

# Sources

The following is a list of sources for the many materials and techniques discussed in this book. Keep in mind that this is only a partial list of the many companies that sell these products. Most of these companies, and many more, advertise in **Rug Hooking** magazine. These companies can get you started with all the supplies you need to finish hand-hooked rugs. The rest is up to you. Enjoy!

**Rug Hooking Magazine**
1300 Market Street, Suite 202
Lemoyne, PA 17043-1420
(800) 233-9055
*www.rughookingonline.com*
*rughook@paonline.com*
The indispensable source of rug hooking information and advertisers. Annual subscription for just $27.95.

**Braid Aid Company**
466 Washington Street
Pembroke, MA 02359
(781) 826-2560
Complete hooking and braiding supplies.

**Cox Enterprises**
10 Dube Road
Verona Island, ME 04416
(207) 469-6402
How-to videos and books on hooking and braiding for beginners and advanced crafters.

**Dorr Mill Store**
Rts. 11 and 103
Guild, NH 03754
(800) 846-3677
*www.dorrmillstore.com*
*dorrmillstore@sugar-river.net*
Quality wools, color palettes, patterns, kits, and much more.

**Fredericksburg Rugs**
231 Rocky Creek Road
PO Box 649
Fredericksburg, TX 78624
(800) 331-5213
*www.fredericksburgrugs.com*
Complete rug hooking supplies.

**Green Mountain Hooked Rugs**
Stephanie Ashworth Krauss
146 Main Street
Montpelier, VT 05602
(802) 223-1333
*vtpansy@together.net*
Patterns, supplies, and the annual Green Mountain Rug School.

**Halcyon Yarn**
12 School Street
Bath, ME 04530
(800) 341-0282
*www.halcyonyarn.com*
High-quality rug yarn for finishing hooked rugs.

**Harry M. Fraser Company**
433 Duggins Road
Stoneville, NC 27048
(336) 573-9830
fraserrugs@aol.com
*www.fraserrugs.com*
Hooking cutters and complete rug
hooking and braiding supplies.

**Heritage Rug Hooking**
13845 Magnolia Avenue
Chino, CA 91710
(909) 591-6351
*www.mcgtextiles.com*
Complete rug hooking and
finishing supplies.

**Hook Nook**
Margaret Siano
1 Morgan Road
Flemington, NJ 08822
(901) 806-8083
*hooknook@ptd.net*
*www.hook-nook.com*
Lib Callaway rug patterns, hooking
supplies, and instructions.

**House of Price, Inc.**
177 Brickyard Road
Mars, PA 16046-3001
(877) RUG-HOOK
*rughook@sgi.net*
Fine quality hooking patterns,
including Charco designs.

**Jane Olson Rug Studio**
PO Box 351
Hawthorne, CA 90250
(310) 643-5902
*www.janeolsonrugstudio.com*
The total rug hooking and braiding supplier for 27 years.

**Patsy B**
Patsy Becker
PO Box 1050, S.
Orleans, MA 02662
(508) 240-0346
*patsyb@c4.net*
Over 250 primitive patterns.

**Pro Chemical & Dye**
PO Box 14
Somerset, MA 02726
(888) 2-BUY-DYE
*www.prochemical.com*
Dyeing supplies.

**Ruckman Mill Farm**
Susan Feller
PO Box 409
Augusta, WV 26704
(908) 832-9565
*www.ruckmanmillfarm.com*
Rug designs by Susan Feller.

**W. Cushing & Company**
PO Box 351
Kennebunkport, ME 04046
(800) 626-7847
*www.wcushing.com*
*rughooks@wcushing.com*
Dyeing supplies, hooks, patterns,
kits, and much more.

**Woolley Fox, LLC**
61 Lincoln Highway East
Ligonier, PA 15658
(724) 238-3004
*www.woolleyfox.com*
Primitive patterns, kits, and
supplies.

**Woolrich**
Catalog Orders
Two Mill Street
Woolrich, PA 17779
(877) 512-7305
(Ask for operator 256)
*rughooking@woolrich.com*
Factory direct rug hooking wool.

## WHAT IS RUG HOOKING?

Some strips of wool. A simple tool. A bit of burlap. How ingenious were the women and men of ages past to see how such humble household items could make such beautiful rugs?

Although some form of traditional rug hooking has existed for centuries, this fiber craft became a fiber art only in the last 150 years. The fundamental steps have remained the same: A pattern is drawn onto a foundation, such as burlap or linen. A zigzag line of stitches is sewn along the foundation's edges to keep them from fraying as the rug is worked. The foundation is then stretched onto a frame, and fabric strips or yarn, which may have been dyed by hand, are pulled through it with an implement that resembles a crochet hook inserted into a wooden handle. The compacted loops of wool remain in place without knots or stitching. The completed rug may have its edges whipstitched with cording and yarn as a finishing touch to add durability.

Despite the simplicity of the basic method, highly intricate designs can be created with it. Using a multitude of dyeing techniques to produce unusual effects, or various hooking methods to create realistic shading, or different widths of wool to achieve a primitive or formal style, today's rug hookers have gone beyond making strictly utilitarian floor coverings to also make wallhangings, vests, lampshades, purses, pictorials, portraits, and more. Some have incorporated other kinds of needlework into their hooked rugs to fashion unique and fascinating fiber art that's been shown in museums, exhibits, and galleries throughout the world.

For a good look at what contemporary rug hookers are doing with yesteryear's craft—or to learn how to hook your own rug—pick up a copy of *Rug Hooking* magazine, or visit our Web site at *www.rughookingonline.com*. Within the world of rug hooking—and *Rug Hooking* magazine—you'll find there's a style to suit every taste and a growing community of giving, gracious fiber artists who will welcome you to their gatherings.—*Wyatt R. Myers*